Every day, I am healing.

My difficulties make me stronger

I'm deserving of love and happiness

I am not my depression

Every breath I take draws me closer to recovery.

I Chose to view the bright side

I am greater than my Struggles

Every day holds the possibility of joy.

I am loved for who I am.

I have the power to change my story.

I am infused with hope and resilience.

My strength is greater than
any obstacle

Tomorrow is a new day with new opportunities

I have the power to create
my happiness.

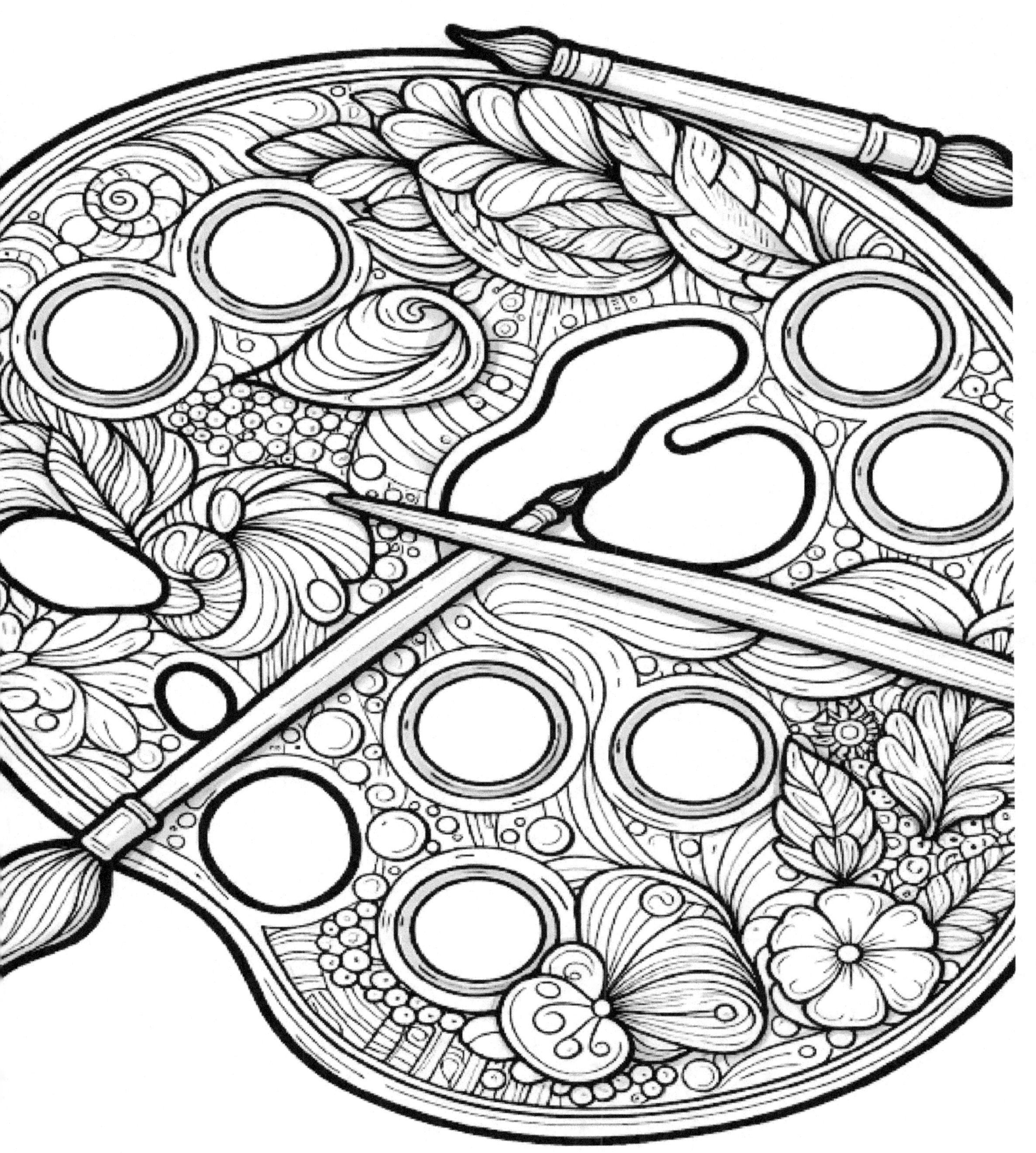

I am worthy of joy and peace.

Challenges are chances to grow.

I believe in my journey and my destiny.

My past does not dictate my future.

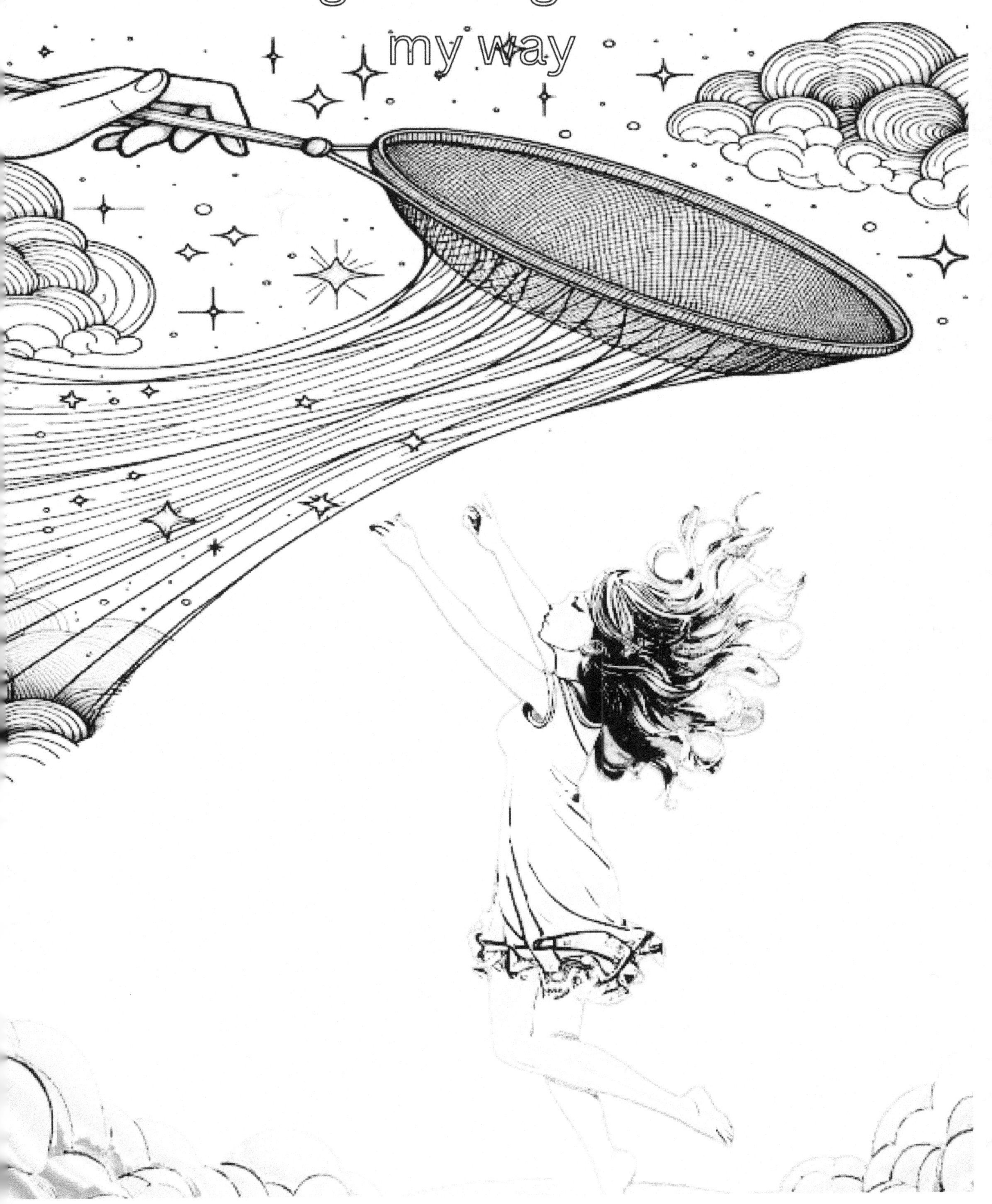

I'm deserving all the good that comes my way

I am in control of my happiness.

I accept the journey with all of its ups and downs

I am not alone in my struggles

I am worth the effort of healing.

Every setback is a setup for a comeback

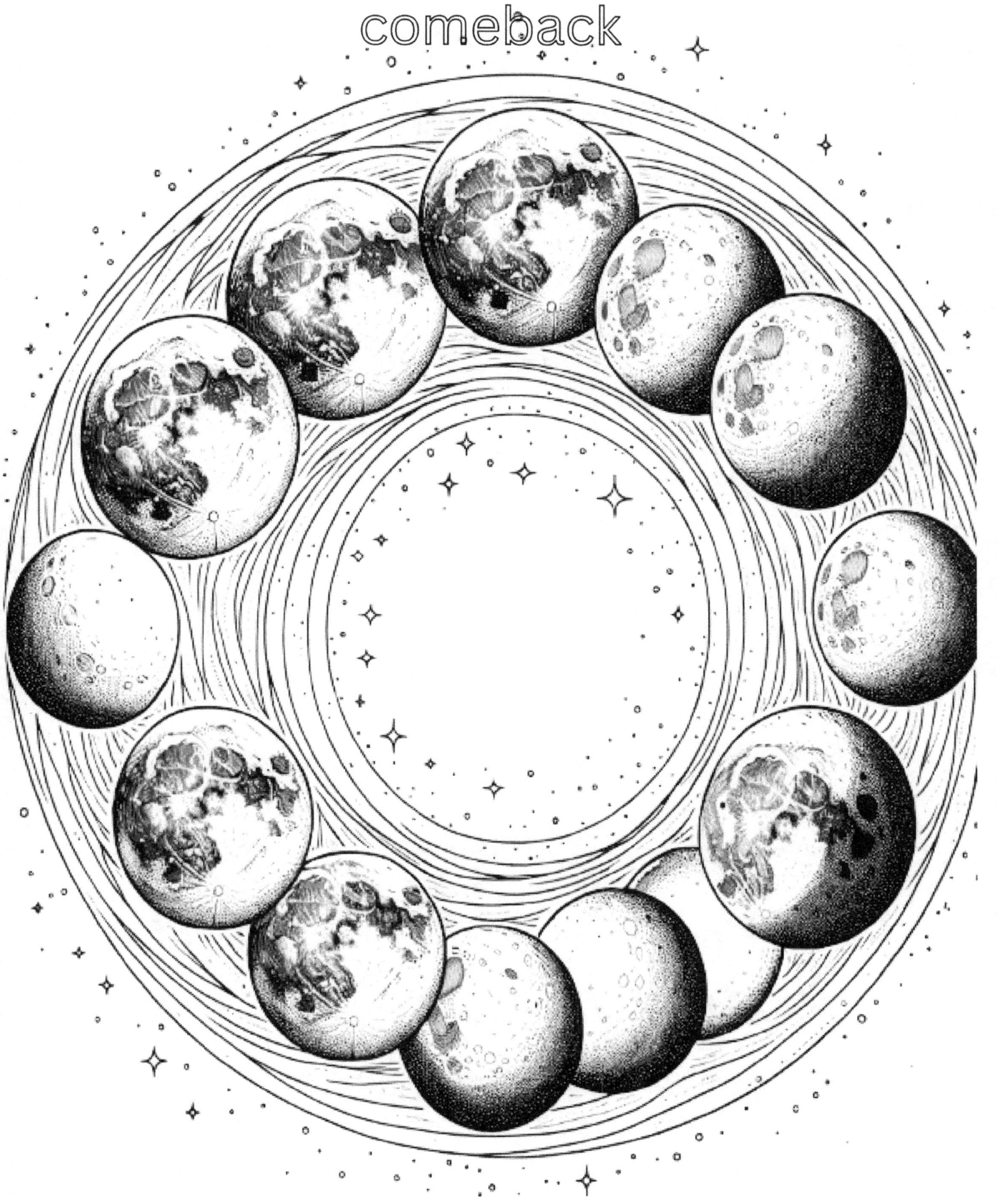

I am constantly growing and evolving.

I find strength in vulnerability.

I trust the journey of self-discovery.

am resilient, like the waves that shape the shore.

Happiness is a choice I make every day

I am deserving of peace and tranquility

My feelings are valid and acknowledged.

I am a beacon of light and positivity.

With every breath, I release my fears.

My self-worth is not determined by others

"I find strength in my challenges

Every day, I become a better version of myself.

I am deserving of every compliment I receive.

With time and patience, I heal.

I embrace the lessons life teaches me

I am my best friend and biggest cheerleader.

I have the power to transform
my life.

I am not defined by my past mistakes

"I choose positivity and optimism.

I choose positivity and optimism

Every challenge brings new opportunities.

I am deserving of all the love
I give and receive.

I focus on my progress, not perfection.

I believe in my ability to overcome.

My voice matters and is heard

I am more than my challenges.